ENGLISCH 3 4

Aufsätze und andere Texte schreiben

Kompetent Aufsteigen ...

3. und 4. Klasse AHS·NMS

Astrid Berger / Gabriele Broniowski

G&G

www.ggverlag.at

ISBN 978-3-7074-1980-1

In der aktuell gültigen Rechtschreibung

1. Auflage 2016

Umschlagillustration: Elena Kratzer
Innenillustrationen: Natasha Chalmers

Printed by Litotipografia Alcione, Lavis-Trento, über Agentur Dalvit, D-85521 Ottobrunn

Inhaltsverzeichnis

Texte schreiben, aber wie?

Nützliche Tipps, die du beachten solltest

In der dritten und vierten Klasse sind viele der Texte, die du schreiben musst, Erzählungen. Daher beziehen sich die folgenden Tipps in erster Linie auf erzählende Texte.

Was ist zu tun?

Englische Texte schreibst du im Moment noch meist für die Schule. Deine Lehrerin oder dein Lehrer erwarten etwas Bestimmtes von dir. Bevor du mit dem Schreiben beginnst, musst du sicher sein, dass du weißt, was du tun sollst.

 Lies die Angabe genau bis zum Ende durch. Wenn dir etwas unklar ist, frag noch einmal nach.

Idee

Es ist nicht sehr klug, wenn du einfach mal drauflosschreibst und darauf vertraust, dass dir beim Schreiben schon irgendetwas einfallen wird. Bevor du beginnst, brauchst du eine Idee. Egal, welche Art von Text du schreibst, er muss interessant sein. Einen langweiligen Text ohne Spannung und Höhepunkt will niemand lesen, auch deine Lehrerin oder dein Lehrer nicht.

 Überlege, bevor du mit dem Schreiben beginnst, und suche nach einer interessanten, spannenden oder lustigen Idee.

Aufbau

Dein Text sollte so aufgebaut sein, dass sich der Leser oder die Leserin gut auskennt. Dein Aufsatz muss eine Einleitung, einen Hauptteil und einen Schluss haben. Diese drei Teile solltest du durch Absätze voneinander trennen.
Nichts ist mühsamer, als einen Text zu lesen, der in einer einzigen endlosen Wurst geschrieben ist. Absätze machen das Lesen leichter, denn sie gliedern deine Erzählung. In einem Absatz stehen Dinge, die inhaltlich zusammengehören. Auch im Hauptteil deines Textes kannst du Absätze machen, immer dann, wenn du etwas Neues zu erzählen beginnst.

 Gliedere deinen Text in Einleitung, Hauptteil und Schluss und vergiss nicht auf die Absätze.

Einleitung – die vier wichtigen „W"

Achte darauf, dass deine Einleitung kurz ist. Du solltest darin schreiben, wer in deinem Text wichtig ist, wo sich die Handlung abspielt, wann das geschieht und eventuell was du erzählen möchtest.

 Bereite deine Leser in der Einleitung darauf vor, wer, wann, wo, was getan hat.

Hauptteil

Der Hauptteil sollte der längste Teil deines Textes sein. Hier erzählst du die eigentliche Geschichte.

Achte darauf, dass du Schritt für Schritt erzählst, was geschieht. Deine Erzählung sollte gegen Ende des Hauptteiles den Höhepunkt erreichen. Das ist der Punkt, an dem die Geschichte am spannendsten oder am lustigsten ist. Hier solltest du sehr genau erzählen.

 Komm am Ende des Hauptteils zum Höhepunkt deiner Geschichte.

Schluss

Der Schlussteil sollte nicht zu lang sein. Hier solltest du alles, was noch unklar ist, erklären und zu einem Ende bringen. Eventuell kannst du auch noch eine überraschende Lösung oder Wende einbauen. Auf alle Fälle muss für den Leser oder die Leserin klar erkennbar sein, dass die Geschichte zu Ende ist.

 Schließe deine Geschichte klar ab.

Titel

Manchmal darfst oder musst du einen Titel für deine Geschichte finden. Er sollte bei der Leserin oder dem Leser Interesse wecken, aber nicht zu viel verraten.

 Finde einen treffenden Titel.

Wenn du mit dem Erzählen fertig bist ...

Wenn deine Geschichte fertig ist, solltest du dir unbedingt Zeit nehmen, um sie in aller Ruhe nochmals durchzulesen. So kannst du Rechtschreib- oder Grammatikfehler entdecken und korrigieren. Je länger die Zeitspanne ist, die zwischen dem Verfassen eines Textes und dem Überarbeiten liegt, desto eher fallen dir Fehler auf.

Achte darauf, dass der neue Text gut leserlich ist. Wenn man deinen Text schlecht oder gar nicht lesen kann, riskierst du, dass deine Lehrerin oder dein Lehrer Fehler anstreicht, weil sie etwas nicht entziffern können.

 Überarbeite deinen Text.

Writing about an event

Kurzer Bericht

Beim Schreiben eines Berichtes solltest du Folgendes beachten:

- Berichte nur über Dinge und Ereignisse, die wirklich passiert sind.
  Ein Bericht ist keine Fantasiegeschichte.
- Beschreibe die wichtigsten Details in einer sinnvollen zeitlichen Abfolge.
- Bei einem Bericht geht es nicht darum, Spannung aufzubauen,
  sondern die Fakten darzustellen.
- Schreibe in der Past Tense.
- Vermeide direkte Reden.
- Vergiss nicht, deinen Text zu gliedern.

Übung

Du findest hier verschiedene Satzanfänge.

Suche dir aus den untenstehenden Wörtern oder Phrasen jeweils eine Möglichkeit aus,

um den Satz zu vervollständigen.

Verwende die Satzanfänge in der vorgegebenen Reihenfolge!

Natürlich kannst du deine Sätze noch etwas ausschmücken.

My holidays

1. This year my summer holidays were …
2. I went to …
3. I went there with my …
4. We went there by …

great	Brighton (England)	parents	car
horrible	Spain	my family	plane
okay	the USA	my best friend	ship
fantastic	Italy	my grandparents	train
awful	Croatia	my brother/sister	coach

5. We stayed in/ with/at ...	6. Every day we went/we had ...	7. The food was ...	8. For breakfast we sometimes had ...
hotel	to the beach to collect shells	okay	black pudding and grilled tomatoes
Bed and Breakfast	riding	yummy	bacon and eggs
a campsite	four English lessons	horrible	French toast
a host family	swimming	awful	waffles
a farm	for a walk along the beach	not as bad as I had expected	porridge

9. For lunch we often had ...	10. For dinner we sometimes had ...	11. In the afternoon/ evening we sometimes went	12. When my summer holidays were over I was really ...
a chicken salad	spaghetti	to the cinema	sorry
some ice cream	beans and egg on toast	on trips	glad
a sandwich	pizza	to the local museum	sad
a hamburger	a steak	to the youth club	angry
fish and chips	sausages and mashed potatoes	to the shopping mall	happy

Dein Text könnte etwa so aussehen:

This year my summer holidays were really great. I went to Brighton, in England. I went there with my best friend Miriam. We went to London by plane and from there we took the train to Brighton. We stayed with a host family. Every day we had four English lessons in the morning. I had to speak a lot of English!
The food was not as bad as I had expected. For breakfast we sometimes had bacon and eggs with toast. For lunch we often just had a sandwich. For dinner we sometimes had pizza. That was really yummy!
In the evening we sometimes went to the cinema. One afternoon we went to the shopping mall and spent a lot of money!
When my summer holidays were over I was really sad because we had to go back to Austria.

Paragraph writing

Kurze Texte schreiben

Ein kurzer Text sollte sich auf eine bestimmte Sache konzentrieren. Narrative (erzählende) Texte beschreiben oft, was eine Person über einen bestimmten Zeitraum hindurch macht oder gemacht hat (z. B. was du letztes Wochenende/in deinen letzten Ferien getan hast, wie dein Tagesablauf aussieht ...).

Deskriptive (beschreibende) Texte schildern oft, wie eine Person/ein Tier aussieht und handelt.

Ein kurzer Text sollte, ähnlich wie ein langer Text, aus Einleitung, Hauptteil und Schluss bestehen. Vergiss nicht, im Hauptteil auf die angegebenen Punkte einzugehen!

Tasks

Mein Tagesablauf am Wochenende

Bevor du mit dem tatsächlichen Text beginnst, solltest du dir Antworten zu folgenden Fragen überlegen. Wähle dazu die Wörter oder Phrasen, die deinen Gewohnheiten am besten entsprechen:

- When do you get up?
  I always/never/sometimes/often get up early/late.

- What do you usually do on a Saturday morning?
  I always/never/sometimes/often have breakfast with my family/meet friends/go to the gym/
  play computer games/watch TV ...

- Do you go to church/the mosque on Friday/Saturday/Sunday?
  Yes/No, I don't go to church/to the mosque on Friday/Saturday/Sunday.

- What do you like doing in your free time?
  I like doing sports/reading books/watching TV/playing computer games/meeting friends/
  listening to music/surfing the Internet/going to parties/going for a walk with my dog ...

Jetzt, da du dir alle Informationen überlegt hast, kannst du mit deinem Paragraph beginnen.
Er könnte so aussehen:

Saturday is often a lazy day for me. On Saturday I usually get up quite late. Sometimes I have breakfast with my family, then I do not eat any lunch. After breakfast I often meet my friends or go to the gym to work out. If the weather is bad I sometimes watch TV or play computer games. In the evening I often go out with my friends. I am allowed to stay out till 11 p.m.
On Sunday I do not go to church although some of my friends do. I love watching TV or reading a book in bed. My mum wants the whole family to have lunch together, so I never get up later than 12 p.m.
In the afternoon I sometimes meet my friends in the park and we play football.
In the evening I usually do some work for school or surf the Internet. As I have to get up early on Monday I never go to bed later than 10 or 11 p.m.

Hier noch ein weiteres Beispiel für einen Paragraph, der nicht erzählend,sondern beschreibend ist.

Many people believe that their cat or dog is very special. Well, my dog Kylie really is different. Firstly, her eyes are each a different colour: one eye is blue, the other one is brown. Her fur is black, grey, white and brown. When people see her they stop and look at her because they have never seen a dog like her.
Secondly, Kylie has a very unusual personality. She loves little dogs and plays with our cat but she is scared when there is a storm. Then she tries to hide under the bed.
Kylie is also a very friendly dog. When people she knows come to visit she licks their hands and sometimes their faces.
I think that you will never find another dog like Kylie.

Nun versuche, kurze Texte zu folgenden Themen zu schreiben:

1. **My last holidays (ca. 120 Wörter)**

   Write about
   • where you went
   • who you went with
   • the best/worst things that happened
   • the wheather

2. **What I did last weekend (ca. 120 Wörter)**

Write about
- how your weekend started
- what you did
- what you liked/didn't like

_____

_____

_____

_____

3. **An (unusual) hobby (100–120 Wörter)**

Write about
- what kind of hobby it is
- why you became interested in it
- how much time you spend on it

_____

_____

_____

_____

4. **A book I read/A film I saw (120–150 Wörter)**

Write about
- the plot (just a few sentences!)
- the characters or actors you liked/disliked
- what you generally (dis)liked about the book/film
- whether you would recommend the book/film

_____

_____

_____

_____

Describing a person

Personenbeschreibung

Wenn du eine Person beschreibst, soll die Leserin oder der Leser sich diese Person auch wirklich vorstellen können. Eine Personenbeschreibung sollte folgende Elemente enthalten:

- Äußere Merkmale: Alter, Größe, Körperbau, Gesicht, Augenfarbe, Haare, Kleidung, besondere Merkmale

- Lebensumstände: Name, Wohnort, Familie, Schule

- Andere Details: Haustiere, Hobbys, Lieblingsbuch, Lieblingsband, Lieblingssängerln, Lieblingsfilm oder –fernsehsendung, Charaktereigenschaften oder die Beziehung zur beschreibenden Person, also zu dir.

- Adjektive (Eigenschaftswörter) spielen bei einer Personenbeschreibung eine ganz wichtige Rolle. Sie helfen dir, Merkmale treffender und genauer darzustellen.
  Beispiele: a tall boy, short curly hair, big blue eyes

Übungen

1. **Ordne folgende Eigenschaftswörter den passenden Spalten zu!**
   Du darfst die einzelnen Wörter auch öfter verwenden.

> slim, fashionable, obese (übergewichtig), good-looking, handsome, old, bald (glatz-köpfig), thin, long, short, big, small, striped, friendly, active, shy, round, beautiful, pretty, boring, fat, modern, colourful, old-fashioned, pale, freckled (mit Sommersprossen), open, braid/plait (Zopf), skinny (sehr mager), curly (gelockt)

body shape	looks (face, eyes, mouth, hair)	clothes	personality

2. Lies die folgende Personenbeschreibung und versuche dann, einen Steckbrief zu erstellen.

My best friend is Hermione. Hermione hates her name, that's why everybody calls her "Minnie". She thinks it is a cool nickname.

Minnie is 13 years old and quite tall for her age. Minnie has long brown hair, which she often wears in a braid/plait, green-brown eyes and a round face. She is slim but not skinny. Most of the time she wears jeans and T-shirts. Her favourite colour is green but she also likes purple and blue. When Minnie wants to look "girlie" she wears a skirt and shoes with low heels (niedriger Absatz).

Minnie lives in a village in Cornwall, England. She lives in a house with a small garden. She shares her room with her twin sister Hannah. Minnie also has a five-year-old brother called Tim, who can sometimes be a pest.

Minnie loves animals, that's why she has three pets: two guinea pigs and a dog. The guinea pigs are called Donald and Daisy and her dog, an Australian shepherd, is called Lilly. Every day in the morning and in the afternoon Minnie takes Lilly for a walk. She plays ball with her dog and teaches her tricks.

Minnie is a good student. Her favourite subject is Maths but she also likes PE very much. As I am not very good at Maths, Minnie often helps me with my Maths homework.

Minnie likes playing the piano and playing tennis. She also loves reading, swimming and riding her bike.

Minnie's favourite singer is Ke$ha but she does not really have a favourite band.

Minnie likes to read vampire stories. Her favourite movies are science fiction and fantasy movies. Whenever she can she watches the Simpsons on TV.

Minnie loves pizza but her mum makes sure that she also eats a lot of fruit and fresh vegetables.

Minnie is a very friendly girl who likes to laugh a lot. I can tell her all my secrets and she never lets me down.

(324 words)

Die folgenden Fragen helfen dir beim Erstellen von Hermiones Steckbrief.
Sie machen es dir leichter, deinen Text zu ordnen und verhindern,
dass du wichtige Details vergisst oder auslässt.

Steckbrief

What is the person's name/nickname? _____

How old is she? _____

How tall is she? _____

What does she look like (body, face, eyes, nose, mouth ...)? _____

_____

How does she wear her hair? _____

What colour is her hair? _____

What kind of clothes does she usually wear? _____

Where does she live? _____

Does she have any brothers and/or sisters? _____

Does she have any pets? _____

What is she good at (at school, outside of school)? _____

What are her hobbies? _____

Who is her favourite band/singer? _____

What is her favourite book/movie/TV series? _____

What is her favourite colour? _____

What is her favourite food/dish? _____

What is special about her? _____

3. **Die folgende Personenbeschreibung ist leider ungeordnet. Verbessere und ergänze die Beschreibung mithilfe der Punkte 1–5! Überlege dir einen guten Schlusssatz!**

> 1. Name/nickname, age, looks (body, face, eyes, hair ...)
> 2. Clothes
> 3. School, family, pets
> 4. Hobbies, favourite band/singer/movie/book/food ... things the person is good at
> 5. Why I like the person, what is special about the person

My friend is called Melanie, and she is 14 years old. She is not very tall. Melanie has long blonde hair with a few red streaks (Strähnen).
Her hobbies are ice skating, reading and playing computer games.
Her favourite food is Indian food. Her favourite dessert is apple pie. She often goes to the cinema with her older brother and her younger sister. They all love fantasy films.
She goes to school by train because she lives in a small village near Baden. She often wears her hair in a ponytail. Melanie is quite slim as she likes doing sports. All her friends call her Melli. In the evening she sometimes chats with her friends on Facebook.
Melli is very friendly and she likes meeting new people. Whenever I need help she is there for me.
Melanie has blue eyes and long eyelashes. She hates her lips because she thinks they are too thin. She often wears skirts and dresses but she also likes to wear jeans. In summer she also wears shorts and sports shoes.

Melli is good at drawing and languages. Her favourite subjects at school are Art, English and Spanish. Melanie loves animals and she has three pets: a rabbit called Arthur, a hamster called Mortimer and a dog called Molly.

Melli lives in a nice little house with her parents and her siblings (Geschwister).

When I visit her we sometimes play with her dog Molly. When it is hot we cool off in their swimming pool.

Melanie plays the saxophone. She does not have a favourite singer or band.

Melli likes to read romantic stories but sometimes she also reads books about vampires. (275 words)

4. Verfasse nun mithilfe der folgenden Fragen und Stichwörter selbst eine Personenbeschreibung!

What is the person's name/nickname?	Robert/Robbie
How old is he/she?	14
How tall is he/she?	170 cm
What does he/she look like (body, face, eyes, nose, mouth ...)?	thin, green eyes, pale face
How does he/she wear his/her hair?	short
What colour is his/her hair?	black
What kind of clothes does he/she usually wear?	jeans and T-shirts, hates: shirts and suits
Where does he/she live?	Liverpool, apartment/flat with balcony
Does he/she have any brothers and/or sisters?	2 brothers/no sister
Does he/she have any pets?	cat (Missy) and dog (Tiger)
What is he/she good at (at school, outside of school)?	good at soccer, bad at German and Art
What are his/her hobbies?	loves swimming and riding, his bike, swim team
Who is his/her favourite band/singer?	Justin Bieber, Black Eyed Peas
What is his/her favourite book/movie/TV series?	action movies, South Park
What is his/her favourite colour?	blue
What is his/her favourite food/dish?	chocolate cake, hates cheese
What is special about him/her?	good friend, helpful, open

Nun versuche, kurze Texte zu folgenden Themen zu schreiben (100–120 Wörter):

1. Describe a member of your family

Write about
- what he or she looks like
- him/her job
- her/his favourite book/movie/band/food/hobby
- what is special about him/her

_____

_____

_____

_____

_____

_____

2. My favourite singer/film star

Write about
- what he/she looks like
- his/her music or films
- why you like him/her

_____

_____

_____

_____

_____

Emails

E-Mails

Bevor du ein E-Mail schreibst, überlege kurz, warum du es schreibst, worum es geht, und welche Art von Antwort oder Reaktion du erwartest. Bevor du ein E-Mail abschickst, solltest du es unbedingt nochmals durchlesen und überprüfen, ob die E-Mail-Adresse stimmt.

1. Informal or personal emails

Sicher schreibst du E-Mails an deine Freunde. Meist achtet man in solch privaten E-Mails nicht auf Rechtschreibung und Grammatikregeln. Auch Abkürzungen und Emoticons (☺☺☹ usw.) sind üblich.

Folgendes solltest du aber beachten, wenn du E-Mails für die Schule als Hausübung oder bei Schularbeiten schreibst:

- Dein E-Mail sollte eine Anrede und einen Schlussgruß enthalten. Bei E-Mails an gute Freunde kannst du „Hi/Hello" oder den Vornamen als Begrüßung verwenden.

- Vermeide extreme Umgangssprache und Slangausdrücke.

- Versuche, dich kurz und klar auszudrücken. Die meisten E-Mails werden am Computer gelesen. Lange Texte am Bildschirm zu lesen, finden viele Menschen mühsam.

- Verwende vollständige Sätze und mach Absätze. Gerade am Bildschirm ist es sehr schwer, ungegliederte Texte, die in einem dahingeschrieben sind, zu lesen.

- Achte, wie in jedem anderen Text auch, auf die Rechtschreibung. Sollte dein E-Mail-Programm eine Rechtschreibprüfung haben, so verwende diese.

- Auch Satzzeichen sind in E-Mails üblich.

- Vergiss nicht, mit deinem Namen zu unterschreiben.

Bausteine, die dir beim Verfassen von E-Mails helfen können:

Als **Einleitung** bei persönlichen E-Mails bieten sich folgende Sätze an:

Many thanks for .../Thank you .../Thanks ...

Just a quick note to let you know ...

Just a few lines ...

I'm writing to ...

I'd like to ...

Examples:

    Hi Sarah,

    I'd like to invite you to my birthday party on Saturday, April 10th.

    Yeah, I'm finally going to be a teenager!

    Ricky,

    Thanks for the birthday wishes!

    Your email was a wonderful surprise.

Dein **Hauptteil** könnte dann eine gute/schlechte Nachricht, die Schilderung eines Problems, eine Entschuldigung oder eine Bitte sein.

Beispiele:

    <u>Freudige Nachricht:</u>

    Guess what! All my studying has finally paid off.

    I got a B on my last English test! Yeah!!

    <u>Schlechte Nachricht:</u>

    I'm afraid (that) I can't come to your birthday party ☹.

    My parents and I are going to London that weekend.

    <u>Anfrage:</u>

    Do you think you could come to my place at the weekend? I really need your advice.

    <u>Entschuldigung:</u>

    I'm sorry I lied to you but I did not know how to tell you the truth.

Dein **Schlusssatz** könnte so aussehen:

    Looking forward to your reply.

    Hope to hear from you soon!

    Enjoy yourself!

    Have a great time!

    See you soon!

Du kannst folgende Bausteine als **Grußformel am Ende** deines E-Mails verwenden:

    Bye,

    Love,

    See you/CU,

    Lots of love,

    Take care!

In persönlichen E-Mails verwenden Teenager, genau wie beim SMS-Schreiben (texting), oft Emoticons und Abkürzungen.

Hier findest du einige Beispiele:

:-)	:-(	;-)	:-o
I'm happy.	I'm unhappy.	just kidding	Wow!

:*)	:-||	:D	:Q
clowning	angry	laughing out loud	What?

asap	as soon as possible
B4	before
BTW	by the way
CU	See you!
FYI	for your information
LOL	laughing out loud
MSG	message
OMG	Oh my God!
pls	please
ROFL	rolling on the floor laughing
sry	sorry
Thx/TX	thanks
xoxox	hugs and kisses

Übung

Finding mistakes

In der folgenden Übung findest du ein E-Mail.

Leider haben sich einige Fehler eingeschlichen. Es sind Vokabelfehler (no/know), Rechtschreibfehler (thing/think), Zeitenfehler (I learn English for three years/I have learned English for three years) und Grammatikfehler (2 year's/2 years).

Das E-Mail stammt von der 14-jährigen Anna, deren Familie für 3 Jahre in die USA gezogen ist und die jetzt eine amerikanische Schule besucht.
Sie schreibt an ihre ehemaligen KlassenkameradInnen.
Ihr E-Mail enthält 20 Fehler, versuche sie zu finden und zu korrigieren.
Am Ende jedes Absatzes findest du die Anzahl, der im Absatz enthaltenen Fehler.

Dear All!
I am here in Orland Park since almost a month now. On my first day at my new school I was really nervos because I didn't now anybody. I was also a bit worry about my accent and I was afraid nobody would understand me. But guess what? Their were a lot of other new kids and a friendly teacher helped us find our classes. My new school is huge and sometimes I still get lost! (7 mistakes)

School hear in America is very different from school in austria. Here the teacher's stay in the classroom and the kids move around. If you need to go to the toilet (they call it bathroom here) you need a hall pass. School starts later then in Austria but we have to stay at school till 3 p.m. The lessons are only 40 instead of 50 minutes. You can also chose some of your classes. I think that is great! (5 mistakes)

We have the same classes every day. Thats sometimes boring but I guess I will get used to the new system soon. After school there are a lots of clubs and activitys. I have joined the volleyball team and I sing in the school choir. As my voice is quiet good I got a part in a musical. I think that's really cool! The clubs and activities have helped my to find much new friends. Of course there are also some bullies at my new school but I try to stay away from them. (6 mistakes)

Guess what? I have also got one of this cool lockers you know from TV! Unfortunately they are not as big as I thought they would be.

I was also surprised to see who clean the school is. I think they clean the floors with big machines every evening. (2 mistakes)

Take care and write back soon!

Anna

Lies dir die folgenden Angaben durch und schreibe dann kurze E-Mails (120–150 Wörter):

1. **You would like to go to the cinema at the weekend and you ask your best friend if she/he would like to come with you.**

   Say
   • when you want to go
   • what kind of film you want to see
   • where you want to see the film

2. **You are in London for four days and you write a quick email to a friend to let him/her know what you have seen/done so far.**

   You should
   • mention where you are staying
   • write about the sights you have already seen
   • write what you like/don't like about London

3. **There is a maths test next week. You write an email to a friend because you need a study buddy (jemand, der mit dir lernt).**

   Say
   • what you need to study
   • when you would like to study
   • why you don't want to study alone

2. Formal emails

Wenn du E-Mails an Leute, die du nicht persönlich kennst oder mit denen du nicht gut befreundet bist, schreibst, gelten zusätzliche Regeln.

- Verwende Standardenglisch und vermeide Kurzformen wie „don't", „isn't" etc.

- Bei einem offiziellen E-Mail verwendest du die Anrede „Dear Sir/Madam" oder „Dear Mr/Mrs" und den Nachnamen der Person. Hinter der Anrede steht ein Beistrich, danach beginnt der Text mit einem großen Anfangsbuchstaben.

- Dein E-Mail sollte wichtige Informationen und notwendige Details enthalten.

- Symbole (☺☺☹ usw.) solltest du in offiziellen E-Mails nicht verwenden.

- Am Ende eines formal emails steht oft ein Schlusssatz, wie z. B. „I am looking forward to your reply."

- Ein formal email beendest du mit „Yours faithfully", wenn du mit „Dear Sir/Madam" begonnen hast. Hast du in der Anrede den Namen verwendet, beendest du das E-Mail mit „Yours sincerely".

- Falls du ein Attachment mitschicken möchtest, vergewissere dich, dass du das Attachment auch angehängt hast.

Übung

Finding mistakes

Dieses E-Mail ist ein Dankbrief von Thomas an seine Gastfamilie, bei der er im Sommer während eines Sprachaufenthaltes gewohnt hat.

Leider finden sich hier zahlreiche Fehler (25). Suche die Fehler und korrigiere sie!

Dear Mr and Mrs O'Hara,

I am now back since three weeks but school started a week ago and so it was not possible for my to write to you earlier. How are you? Are you busy as usually? Do you have any new guests? (4 mistakes)

I am miss you and all my friends from the language school a lots! We had so much fun together! Thank you for treating me as a member of your family. How is Misty, my favourite dog? Does he still try to steal some food that you don't put away but live on the kitchen table? (5 mistakes)

Last week I have got a email from my Italian friend Guilia (Remind Guilia? She stayed with your neighbours.). Like me she is still in contact with some of the boys and girls from my language class. I was lucky because I made so much good friends during I was in England.

It was really interesting to meet peoples from all over the world. As I had to speak a lot of english I think my spoken English has improved a lot (unfortunately I still have problems with my written English). (7 mistakes)

My parents, my brother and my sister are all fine. My sister will take her A-level exams this year, so we are all very exciting. My brother is still crazy about football and he is now playing in a football team! My mum is worry that he has not enough time to study for school! (3 mistakes)

By the way, I think I left a jean and a T-shirt in the cupboard of my room. Could you please send them to me? Please let us know who much money you payed for shipping my clothes. (3 mistakes)

Please write soon. My parents send there regards. I hope I can come back again next year. I really loved staying with you. Thank you for all things! I hope there are not to many mistakes in this letter. (3 mistakes)

Yours sincerely,

Thomas

Lies dir die folgenden Angaben durch und schreibe dann ein E-Mail (120–150 Wörter):

1. **Your parents are very strict and even though you are already 14 you are not allowed to stay out later than 9 p.m. (not even at weekends). You write to a youth magazine to ask for advice.**

   You should
   • describe the problem
   • say how you feel about the situation
   • ask what could or should do/not do

2. **Read the job advertisement and write a letter of application.**

   You are looking for a summer job?
   You like children and know how to handle them?
   Your English is quite good?
   You are over 15?

   Then you should write to us. We are looking for young people to help us at our English summer camp.
   Write to: Emily Jackson, 5340 St. Gilgen, Hauptplatz 5

Picture stories

Bildgeschichten

Beim Schreiben einer Bildgeschichte musst du die Geschichte, die in den Bildern dargestellt wird, mit deinen Worten erzählen. Folgende Dinge solltest du dabei beachten:

- Schau dir zuerst die Bilder gut an und überlege dir, was in den einzelnen Bildern geschieht. Achte auf Einzelheiten!

- Lass, bevor du zu schreiben beginnst, die Handlung wie einen kleinen Film vor deinem geistigen Auge ablaufen.

- Überlege dir einen Ort und einen Zeitpunkt, an dem das Beschriebene geschehen sein könnte.

- Was könnte vorher und nachher passiert sein?

- Beachte, dass eine Bildgeschichte keine Bildbeschreibung ist.
  Du musst daher auch erzählen, was zwischen den Bildern geschieht.
  Ein oder zwei Sätze über jedes Bild sind noch keine Bildgeschichte!

- Halte dich bei deiner Erzählung an die Reihenfolge der Bilder,
  da sich sonst eventuell der Inhalt verändert.

- Gib den handelnden Personen Namen und beschreibe sie. Stell dir vor, was sie denken und wie sie sich fühlen und versuche, das in deiner Geschichte auszudrücken.
  Um den Text lebendiger zu machen, kannst du die direkte Rede verwenden.

- Achte darauf, dass du beim Erzählen nicht die Zeiten wechselst.

- Deine Geschichte sollte so klar geschrieben sein, dass man die Handlung versteht, ohne die Bilder zu kennen.

Tasks

Schreibe zu den folgenden Bildern eine Geschichte und verwende dabei die angegebenen Eigenschaftswörter (manchmal kannst du natürlich auch das Adverb nehmen)!

sunny – happy – worried – afraid – busy – quick – loud – deep – near – slow

Continue the story

Fortsetzungsgeschichte

Eine Fortsetzungsgeschichte schreibst du im Prinzip wie jede Erzählung, nur hast du bereits einen Anfang vorgegeben.

Folgendes solltest du beachten:

- Lies dir den Beginn der Geschichte gut durch und achte auf die Personen, die vorkommen, auf Orts- und Zeitangaben.

- Achte darauf, ob es sich um eine Ich- oder Er-/Sie-Erzählung handelt, denn so musst du dann auch weitererzählen.

- Überlege, wie die Geschichte weitergehen könnte, ob es in dem Text, an den du anschließt, inhaltliche Hinweise gibt. Diese müsstest du nämlich in deiner Fortsetzung beachten.

- Achte darauf, dass du schon einen Plan deiner Geschichte im Kopf hast, bevor du zu schreiben beginnst. „Es wird schon irgendwie weitergehen." ist keine gute Strategie.

Tasks

**Setze die folgenden Geschichten fort und beachte dabei die Tipps,
die du gerade gelesen hast.**

1. When Peter looked out of the window he couldn't believe his eyes. There was a strange object right in front of his window. It was yellow and green and looked like a miniature spaceship. "What the heck is this?" he thought. "Sandy, come here! Look!" he shouted.

2. It was a sunny spring day. Mrs Hill was taking her dog Buster for a walk when he suddenly started barking like mad. "What is it, boy?" Mrs Hill said. Buster looked at her and pulled her towards some bushes. When Mrs Hill looked more closely she saw a hand sticking out of the ground.

Writing a story from prompts

Reizwortgeschichte

Diese Textform kennst du aus dem Deutschunterricht. Mithilfe von vorgegebenen Wörtern sollst du eine sinnvolle Geschichte erfinden.

Wichtig: Es geht nicht darum, möglichst viele der Wörter in möglichst wenigen Sätzen unterzubringen! Auch eine Reizwortgeschichte soll interessant und spannend zu lesen sein.

- Lies zuerst die angegebenen Wörter durch und überlege dir dann eine sinnvolle Geschichte dazu.

- Meist hat deine Lehrerin oder dein Lehrer die Wörter so gewählt, dass sie in einem gewissen Zusammenhang stehen. Die Reihenfolge, in der du die Wörter in deine Geschichte einbaust, ist egal. Du musst aber alle Wörter verwenden.

- Wie bei jeder Erlebniserzählung solltest du in der Einleitung die wichtigsten Informationen zum Verständnis der Geschichte geben. (Wer sind die handelnden Personen? Wo und wann hat sich das Geschehen abgespielt? ...)

- Im Hauptteil erzählst du das eigentliche Ereignis und führst die Handlung zu einem Höhepunkt.

- Vergiss nicht darauf, deine Geschichte zu einem richtigen Ende zu bringen. Ein Schlusssatz kann noch einmal kurz zusammenfassen oder einen Ausblick geben. **Tipp:** Nicht jede Geschichte muss damit enden, dass die Hauptperson aufwacht und alles nur ein Traum war. Die meisten Lehrerinnen und Lehrer finden ein solches Ende mittlerweile ein bisschen einfallslos!

Tasks

Verwende die folgenden Wörter, um jeweils eine Geschichte zu schreiben.

1. camping holiday in Australia, bush fire, tent, get lost, scared, kangaroo, rescue plane, happy

2. skateboard, friends, dangerous jumps, competition, fall, no helmet, concussion (Gehirnerschütterung), hospital, parents angry and happy

3. burglar, steal, window, diamond ring, noise, wake up, gun, rope, police, prison

4. New York, sightseeing, museum, locked in, scared, mobile phone, problems with English, hotel, enjoy

Adventure/Mystery/Fantasy stories

Abenteuer-, Kriminal- und Fantasiegeschichte

Wie schon der Name sagt, sollten diese Texte spannende Elemente enthalten.
Das bedeutet, dass du dir, bevor du zu schreiben anfängst, die Handlung deiner Geschichte
sehr genau überlegen musst.

Schreib dir Stichwörter auf und sammle Ideen!

Deine Vorbereitung könnte etwa so aussehen:

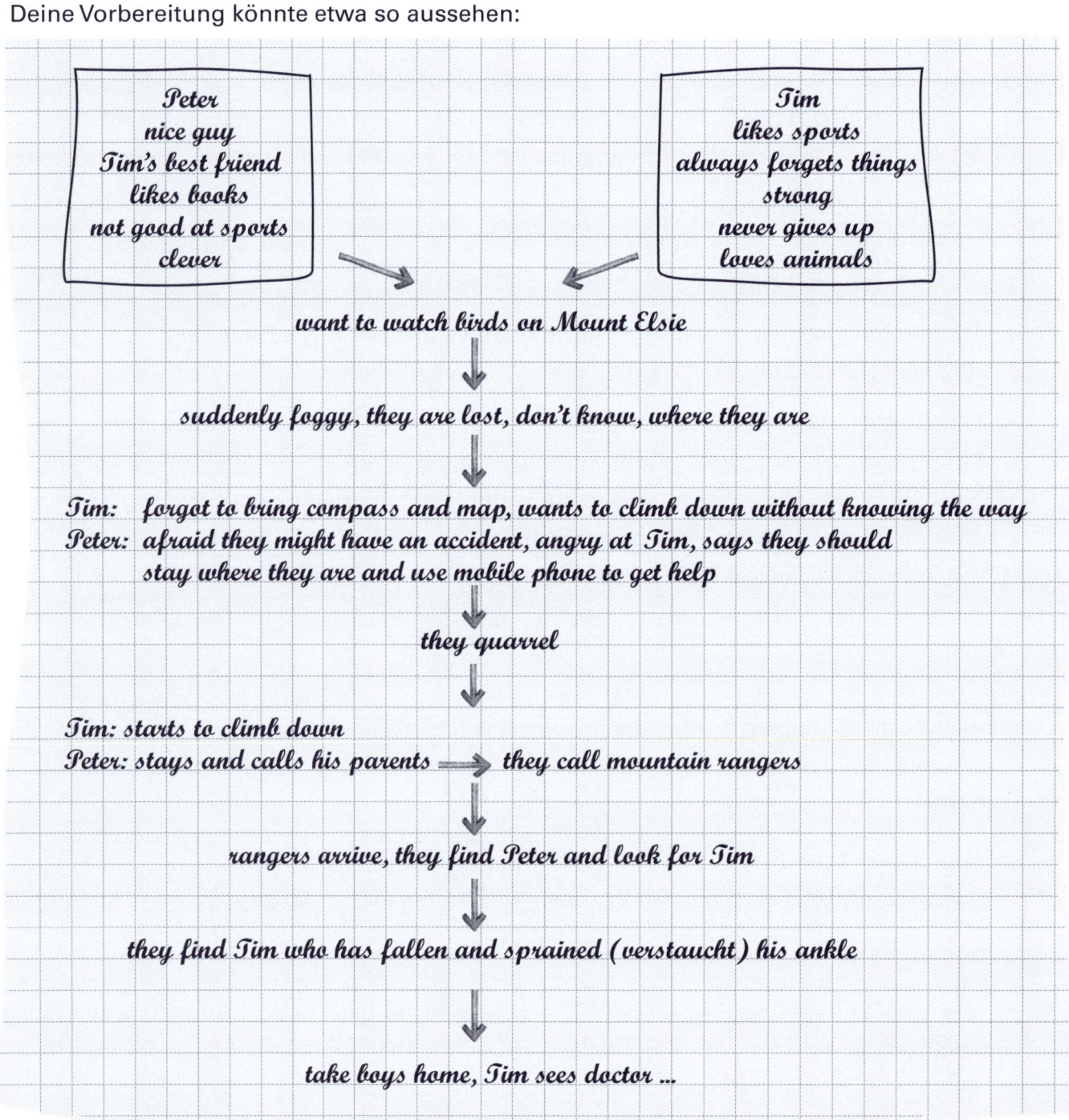

Peter
nice guy
Tim's best friend
likes books
not good at sports
clever

Tim
likes sports
always forgets things
strong
never gives up
loves animals

want to watch birds on Mount Elsie

suddenly foggy, they are lost, don't know, where they are

Tim: forgot to bring compass and map, wants to climb down without knowing the way
Peter: afraid they might have an accident, angry at Tim, says they should
stay where they are and use mobile phone to get help

they quarrel

Tim: starts to climb down
Peter: stays and calls his parents ——→ they call mountain rangers

rangers arrive, they find Peter and look for Tim

they find Tim who has fallen and sprained (verstaucht) his ankle

take boys home, Tim sees doctor ...

- Achte darauf, dass die Geschichte nicht zu unwahrscheinlich wird (außer natürlich, du schreibst gerade eine Fantasiegeschichte). Dein Text sollte glaubwürdig und echt wirken.

- Wenn du deine Ideen gesammelt und organisiert hast, beginne mit dem Schreiben.

- Achte auf die Gliederung in Einleitung, Hauptteil und Schlussteil.
Der Hauptteil sollte am längsten sein, denn er erzählt die eigentliche Geschichte.
Einteilung und Schlussteil sind kürzer.

- Vergiss nicht darauf, Absätze zu machen.

Tasks

Schreibe mithilfe des obigen Stichwortzettels eine spannende Geschichte!

_____

_____

_____

_____

_____

_____

_____

_____

_____

_____

_____

_____

Fairy tale

Märchen

Wenn du ein Märchen schreibst, solltest du einige Dinge über Märchen wissen:

- Märchen spielen nicht an einem bestimmten geografischen Ort und nicht zu einer bestimmten Zeit.

- Ein englisches Märchen beginnt so: Once upon a time there ...

- Meist enden englische Märchen so: And they lived happily ever after.

- Häufig spielen Märchen in einem Schloss, im Wald, bei einem Brunnen, an einem Königshof ...

- Oft kommen folgende Figuren in einem Märchen vor: König, Königin, Prinzessin, Prinz, Zauberer, Hexe, Fee, Zwerg, Riese, Bauer ...

- Zahlen spielen eine bedeutende Rolle, z. B. drei, sieben ...

- Oft geht es in Märchen um den Kampf zwischen Gut und Böse, das Gute siegt am Ende.

- Gute Menschen werden am Ende belohnt, böse werden – manchmal sehr grausam – bestraft.

- Tiere können sprechen, Dinge und Pflanzen haben oft besondere Kräfte.

Übung

Vervollständige die Sätze mit den Linking Words aus der Box!
Verwende jedes Linking Word nur einmal!

Part 1
The three magic nuts

at first – when – suddenly – then – and – because – while – when

Once upon a time there was a poor family. The farmer and his wife had three sons and a daughter. The daughter was called Happy _____ she was friendly and always made her brothers laugh.

One day the father said, "All our money is gone _____ we have nothing to eat. I have to go to the castle and try to find work. Maybe the king needs a hunter."

Happy's three brothers went with their father. They hoped that they would also find work at the castle.

_____ her father and her brothers were gone Happy went into the wood to collect firewood. _____ she saw something shining in the grass. _____ she went closer she saw that the shining thing was a golden nut. _____ she picked it up she saw two more golden nuts lying in the grass. Happy could not believe her luck. She took the nuts and ran home.

She showed the nuts to her mother. _____ they did not know what to do with the nuts. _____ Happy had an idea.

"Maybe they are magic nuts. Let's open them and see what is inside."

Part 2

Lies den 2. Teil des Märchens! Wo gehören die Sätze und Satzteile a–g im Text hin?

When Happy opened the first nut she suddenly heard a voice: "Eat the nut, then make a wish." (1) _____ The nuts were indeed magic!

First Happy wanted a nice house for her family and herself, (2) _____ for all of them. When eating the third nut she asked for happiness.

When Happy's father and brothers came home they were very tired and sad because they had not found any work at the castle. When they came to the place (3) _____ they could not believe their eyes. What had happened? Happy told them about the three magic nuts and what she had wished for. They thanked her, (4) _____ , enough food, and they were happy.

When the neighbour found out about the three magic nuts he was really angry. He thought that he would have made better use of the nuts. (5) _____ Maybe he would also find some magic nuts. Well, he did indeed find three magic nuts! When he came home he opened them, ate them and made his wishes: (6) _____ , he wanted to be rich, and he wanted to be powerful. When he lived in his palace he felt very lonely. He also had money but he did not know who he could trust. He also had power but he did not have a lot of friends. He was very unhappy. The farmer and his family, on the other hand, had made good wishes (7) _____ .

a) and they lived happily ever after.

b) because now they had a nice house

c) Happy was really excited.

d) He decided to go into the wood too.

e) He wanted to live in a palace

f) then she wanted enough food

g) where their old house had been

Book report

Buchbesprechung

Vielleicht bist du eine/r der Schülerinnen oder Schüler, die nicht sehr gerne lesen. Wahrscheinlich möchte deine Lehrerin oder dein Lehrer aber, dass du zumindest ein Buch pro Semester/Jahr liest und darüber schreibst.
Die folgenden Fragen sollen dir helfen, dich bei deinem Book report auf das Wesentliche zu konzentrieren.

Title of the book:	
Author(s) of the book:	
What is the **main idea** or **theme** of this book?	
What is the **setting** of the book? **What year** is it? **Where** does the **action** take place? **What time of year** is it? Start with a **general description** and **then** become **more specific**.	
Who is the **main character** in the story?	
Give a **physical description** of the main character! What does he/she look like?	
Give a description of the **main character's personality**!	
Name some **other characters**!	Give a description of these characters!
Which **character** is your **favourite**?	
Give 2–3 **reasons why**!	
What is the **mood** or **tone** of the story? **How** does it **make you feel** when you read it?	
What happens in the **conclusion** of the book? How does the **story end**?	
What did you **like** or **dislike** about this book?	
Would you **recommend** this book to someone else? **Why or why not**?	

Hier nun ein Beispiel, wie du den Raster ausfüllen könntest.

Title of the book: Harry Potter and the Philosopher's Stone
Author(s) of the book: J. K. Rowling
What is the **main idea** or **theme** of this book? about a boy who has magic powers, Harry's first year at Hogwarts (school for magicians), Harry's adventures at Hogwarts
What is the **setting** of the book? **What year** is it? **Where** does the **action** take place? **What time of year** is it? Start with a **general description** and then become **more specific**. life with the Dursleys (Harry's uncle, aunt and cousin), life at Hogwarts; action takes place in Little Whinging (Surrey), London and at Hogwarts; time: present; time of year: summer and autumn; why Harry lives with Dursleys, Harry's life with the Dursleys, how they treat him; Harry's first year at Hogwarts (lessons, friends, problems ...)
Who is the **main character** in the story? Harry
Give a **physical description** of the main character! What does he/she look like? small and skinny, thin face, black unruly hair, bright-green eyes, thin scar on forehead (Stirn) – shaped like bolt of lightning (Blitz); wears cousin's old clothes, his glasses held together with Sellotape (Tixo)
Give a description of the **main character's personality**: shy at first, curious, brave, friendly

Name some **other characters**	Give a description of some of these characters!
Ron Weasley, Hermione Granger, Draco Malfoy, Dumbledore, Hagrid, Voldemort, Professor Snape, Vernon, Dudley and Petunia Dursley	Ron: red hair, comes from big family, friendly Hermione: ambitious (ehrgeizig), clever, muggle parents (no magicians) Draco Malfoy: schoolmate, does not like Harry, arrogant Hagrid: keeper of keys and grounds at Hogwarts, giant, loves animals Dumbledore: headmaster at Hogwarts, very intelligent, great magician Dursleys: Harry's relatives, took him in when his parents died

Which character is your **favourite**? Harry
Give 2–3 **reasons why**: has magic powers but he is still an ordinary boy; friendly and helpful, not arrogant although survived an attack by Voldemort (evil magician)

What is the **mood** or **tone** of the story? How does it make you feel when you read it? you feel sorry for Harry, Dursleys treat him badly; part where Harry is at Hogwarts ▸ exciting, would like to be at Hogwarts too
What happens in the **conclusion** of the book? How does the **story end**? Harry fights against Voldemort (his body destroyed but evil spirit survived), wants Philosopher's Stone, Harry wins fight, saved by Professor Dumbledore
What did you **like** or **dislike** about this book? liked the way story was told, good descriptions of characters;
Would you recommend this book to someone else? Yes, I liked it.

Mithilfe deiner Antworten kannst du nun eine Inhaltsangabe des Buches schreiben.
Anschließend an die Inhaltsangabe werden die einzelnen Charaktere näher beschrieben.
Zum Schluss solltest du deine persönliche Meinung über das Buch zum Ausdruck bringen.

All das könnte etwa so aussehen:

Summary

Harry Potter and the Philosopher's Stone is a book by J. K. Rowling.

The story is about a boy whose parents were killed and who is brought up by his uncle
and aunt. Harry does not know that he is a wizard and that he has magic powers although
sometimes he suspects (vermuten) that he is different than his relatives (sometimes strange
things happen, e.g. once his aunt cut his hair and the next day it had grown back!).

For ten years Harry lives with his relatives who treat him badly. He has to live in the cupboard
under the stairs, he has to wear Dudley's old clothes although they are much too big for him,
and he never gets any presents.

One day Harry gets a letter from Hogwarts, the School of Witchcraft and Wizardry. The letter
tells him that he has been accepted by the school and that school will start on September 1st.
The Dursleys do not want to let Harry go but Hagrid, a giant who works at Hogwarts, comes
to get Harry.

Harry and Hagrid go to Gringotts, the wizards' bank to get money, then they go to Diagon
Alley to buy the things Harry will need at Hogwarts.

On the train to Hogwarts Harry meets Ron Weasley and Hermione Granger who later become
two of his best friends.

At the school Dumbledore, the headmaster, welcomes the students before they are "sorted".
At Hogwarts there are four houses – Gryffindor, Hufflepuff, Ravenclaw and Slytherin – and
Harry, Ron and Hermione are put into Gryffindor.

Right from the start Professor Snape, the Potions Master, does not like Harry very much. He
believes Harry is treated better than the other students because he survived an attack by
Voldemort, the evil wizard.

Draco Malfoy, a fellow schoolmate, also hates Harry because he is famous. He tries to get him expelled but his plan does not work out.

Harry is accepted into the Quidditch team, a sport played by wizards, and becomes the youngest seeker in the history of Hogwarts.

When Harry, Hermione and Ron hear the name Nicholas Flamel they try to find out who he was and they discover that he was the maker of the Philosopher's Stone. It is a substance that will change any metal into gold and it also produces an elixir that makes the drinker immortal (unsterblich).

When looking for the stone the three friends find a trap door. They open it and climb in. There are several problems they have to overcome but in the end Harry wins against Voldemort with the help of his two friends, Ron and Hermione. Dumbledore destroys the Philosopher's Stone.

It is the end of the school year and Harry has to go back to the Dursleys.

Eine nähere Beschreibung eines Charakters könnte so aussehen:

Harry

Harry is a ten-year-old boy who lives with his uncle, his aunt and his cousin. His parents are dead. Harry is small and skinny for his age, and he has black unruly hair and bright-green eyes. He also has a scar on his forehead that looks like a bolt of lightning. He has to wear his cousin's old clothes although they are much too big for him. He has to live in the cupboard under the stairs and his relatives do not treat him like a member of the family.

Harry is an intelligent and brave boy. He is not extremely ambitious. He is always there for his friends and helps people who have problems.

When Harry goes to Hogwarts his life changes. He finds friends – Ron and Hermione – and he becomes a member of the school's Quidditch team. He is the youngest seeker ever.

He also has enemies: his Potions Teacher, Professor Snape, and his schoolmate Draco Malfoy.

In the end, Harry finds the Philosopher's Stone and wins a confrontation with Voldemort.

Ein Absatz über deine persönliche Meinung könnte etwa so aussehen:

I liked the book because I like stories about wizards and magic. I especially liked the part about Hogwarts because it is very different from my school.

My favourite character was Harry because he is clever and brave (mutig).

I would definitely recommend the book, especially if you like to read about witches, wizards, magic and exciting adventures.

Filling in a form

Ein Formular ausfüllen

Stell dir vor, du möchtest im Sommer an einem Sprachkurs in England oder Irland teilnehmen und während dieser Zeit bei einer Gastfamilie wohnen. Die Organisation, die deinen Sprachaufenthalt betreut, braucht dafür einige Informationen von dir.
Das folgende Formular ist ein Beispiel, wie so ein Formular aussehen könnte.

Wahrscheinlich wirst du nicht alle Ausdrücke in diesem Formular verstehen.
Daher findest du im Anschluss eine kurze Liste von nützlichen Vokabeln, die du beim Ausfüllen des Formulars brauchen kannst.

sex/gender	Geschlecht
M/F (male/female)	männlich/weiblich
dd/mm/yyyy	Tag/Monat/Jahr
to object to something	etwas ablehnen
country of residence	Land, in dem du wohnst
postal code/zip code	Postleitzahl
landline	Festnetz
purpose	Zweck
host family	Gastfamilie
to be hosted by somebody	bei jemandem als Gast untergebracht sein
requirements and restrictions	Anforderungen und Einschränkungen
concerning	betreffend

1. PERSONAL DATA

First Name: _____

Family Name/Surname: _____

Sex/Gender: ☐ M   ☐ F

Date of Birth (dd/mm/yyyy): _____

Religion: _____

Nationality: _____

Home address (line 1): _____

Home address (line 2): _____

City, Town: _____

Postal code/zip code: _____

Country of residence: _____

Home phone (landline): _____

Mobile phone: _____

Email address: _____

2. NEXT OF KIN/EMERGENCY CONTACT PERSON

First name: _____

Family name: _____

Complete address (including country etc.):

Home phone (landline): _____

Mobile phone: _____

Email address: _____

3. PERSONAL HABITS AND PREFERENCES

Animals:

Do you like animals? ☐ yes ☐ no

To which animals do you object?

_____

4. YOUR SPARE TIME/HOBBIES

Describe your spare time activities/your hobbies:

_____

_____

_____

5. TRAVEL EXPERIENCE

Which foreign countries, if any, have you visited? For how long and for what purpose?

_____

_____

Have you ever been a guest in the home of a foreign family? When and for how long?

_____

_____

_____

_____

6. STAYING WITH A HOST FAMILY

Would you mind sharing a room with another student?   ☐ yes   ☐ no

Would you prefer to be hosted by a   ☐ large or a   ☐ small family?

7. INFORMATION CONCERNING HEALTH

Do you have any special requirements or restrictions concerning your health?
If yes, what are they?

_____

_____

Do you have to take any medication regularly?   ☐ yes   ☐ no

If so, which medication? _____

How often? _____ Why? _____

Do you suffer from an allergy?   ☐ yes   ☐ no

What kind of allergy? _____

What must be done in case of an allergy attack? _____

Do you have to follow a special diet? If so, please describe:

_____

_____

Pros and cons

Einfache Erörterung

Manchmal musst du im Englischunterricht über ein bestimmtes Thema schreiben und
Argumente für oder gegen eine Sache finden.
Dabei ist es wichtig beide Seiten darzustellen.
Natürlich darfst du aber deine eigene Meinung vertreten.
Wenn du über die Pros und Cons schreibst, solltest du Folgendes beachten:

- Im ersten Absatz stelltst du dein Thema vor, das heißt, du erklärst, über welches Problem
  du schreiben wirst.
  Dabei kannst du deine persönliche Meinung schon zum Ausdruck bringen.
  Beispiel: "I think teenagers should not be allowed to smoke."

- Der zweite Absatz sollte dein stärkstes Argument enthalten.
  Es begründet deine Meinung.
  Hier kannst du auch Beispiele aus dem täglichen Leben anführen.
  Beispiel: "Smoking is dangerous for people's health."

- Weitere Argumente, die deine Meinung unterstützen, behandelst du in jeweils
  einem eigenen Absatz.
  Beispiel: "Cigarettes are very expensive."

- Gehe nun auf die Gegenargumente ein.
  Beispiele: "Everybody should be allowed to do what he/she wants.",
  "All my friends smoke. Why shouldn't I?", "Smoking helps you to relax."

- Jetzt erklärst du, warum du die Gegenargumente ablehnst.

- Am Schluss fasse nochmals die Gründe für deine Meinung zusammen.

- Folgende Phrasen kannst du in einen solchen Text einbauen:

I think	ich glaube
in my opinion	meiner Meinung nach
for instance	zum Beispiel
on the one hand	einerseits
on the other hand	anderseits
one advantage is that	ein Vorteil ist, dass
finally	schließlich

Tasks

Beispieltext:

Should teenagers smoke?

Pros	**Cons**
helps to relax	bad for your health
makes you feel cool	costs a lot of money
all my friends smoke	smokers smell awful

Nowadays a lot of teenagers smoke. During the breaks there is always a group of older students, who smoke a cigarette, in front of our school. I think that smoking is a bad habit (Gewohnheit).

Smoking is bad for your health. People who smoke a lot often have a bad cough (Husten) and some of them even die from lung or heart diseases (Krankheiten).

Cigarettes are also very expensive. I think it is stupid to spend all one's pocket money on cigarettes. There are so many nice things you can buy instead.

Another reason why I hate smoking is the smell. In my opinion smokers smell terrible. When you spend an evening with people who smoke a lot your clothes still smell awful the next morning.

My friends who smoke often say that smoking helps them to relax. Well, I think I can relax very well without a cigarette. Many teenagers think that they are cool if they smoke. Some smoke because all the people in their group do. In my opinion it is much cooler not to do what everybody else does.

I think everybody should decide if he or she wants to smoke or not. Young people should take care of their health and try to find other ways of being cool.

Mache eine Liste der Pros und Cons zu den folgenden Themen und schreibe dann einen Text:

1. Should school last from 8.00 a.m. to 4.00 p.m.?

Write about
- the advantages/disadvantages of a later start
- the effects on students' free time
- the consequences for students who live far away from school

_____

_____

_____

_____

_____

_____

2. Should 13/14-year-olds be allowed to stay out till 1.00 at night?

Write about
- the dangers of staying out late at that age
- transport problems
- your parents' opinion

_____

_____

_____

_____

_____

3. Should tests be abolished (abgeschafft)?

Write about
- why tests are necessary/unnecessary
- the stress tests cause
- alternative forms of testing students' knowledge

_____

_____

_____

_____

_____

Summary

Zusammenfassung oder kurze Nacherzählung

Wenn du eine Zusammenfassung schreibst, solltest du folgende Punkte beachten:

- Lies den Text aufmerksam durch und überlege dir, was der wesentliche Inhalt ist.

- Finde heraus, was du weglassen kannst und was du schreiben musst, damit deine Zusammenfassung für den Leser oder die Leserin verständlich ist und man der Geschichte gut folgen kann.

- Halte dich beim Schreiben an die Abfolge der Handlung, wie sie im ursprünglichen Text vorkommt.

- Drücke dich klar und eindeutig aus.
  Ausschmückende Eigenschaftswörter sind in einer Zusammenfassung nicht nötig.

- Deine eigene Meinung soll in einer Zusammenfassung nicht vorkommen.
  Du erzählst nur kurz den Inhalt des Textes nach.

Tasks

Fasse den folgenden Text in nicht mehr als 100 Wörtern zusammen!
Im Lösungsteil findest du ein Beispiel, wie so eine Zusammenfassung aussehen könnte.

The story of St. Patrick

St. Patrick, the patron saint of Ireland, lived at the end of the 4th and the beginning of the 5th centuries. He was born in Wales. When he was fourteen years old he was taken to Ireland as a slave. For six years he had to work very hard on a farm. He often prayed to God and one night God told him that he had to escape. Patrick managed to get to a port where he asked the captain of a ship transporting wolfhounds to France to take him on board. The captain didn't want to have a slave on his ship and sent Patrick away. But when the ship was about to leave the pier the hounds began to bark and to behave like mad. So the ship had to return. When they tried again later the same thing happened. Now Patrick saw his chance. He told the captain that he would calm the dogs if the captain took him to France. The captain agreed and really, when Patrick boarded the ship the hounds became quiet. So Patrick got to France and from there back to his family in Wales.

Soon Patrick found out that he wanted to become a priest. Later he returned to Ireland to become a missionary. It was Easter when he arrived in Ireland. Patrick and the other priests, who had come with him, decided that they wanted to light a fire. That night was also a very special night for the Irish people who were no Christians. They were celebrating the coming of spring. Usually their king lit a fire as a sign for all the other people to light their fires. But now Patrick had lit his fire first. The Irish king was very angry and sent people to put out Patrick's fire but they couldn't. Only Patrick could do it.

Soon Patrick began to talk to the people. They were surprised that he could speak their language so very well. He told them about the Christian God and about Jesus.

So he brought Christianity to Ireland.

A legend says that Patrick drove the snakes from Ireland. He was standing on a hill and with a wooden stick drove the snakes into the sea. There are really no snakes in Ireland but this may be because Ireland is an island separated from the continent, so the snakes could not get there. Besides, snakes were a common symbol in many old Irish religions.

The story of St. Patrick and the snakes is a symbol of Christianity replacing pagan (heidnisch) religions in Ireland.

Each year on March 17th the Irish all over the world celebrate St. Patrick's Day.

(449 words)

_____

_____

_____

_____

_____

_____

_____

_____

_____

_____

_____

_____

_____

_____

Fasse den folgenden Text in nicht mehr als 50 bis 70 Wörtern zusammen!

The bake sale

Tony's football team/soccer team needed money to buy new uniforms. They decided to have a bake sale (Kuchenverkauf) before their next game to raise the money (Geld aufbringen). Everyone on the team had to bring something to sell. Tony was planning to bake blueberry muffins with his dad.

On the morning of the sale Tony and his dad got up early because they wanted to have enough time to bake the muffins. While the muffins were in the oven, Tony played with a football in the garden. When the oven timer buzzed (summen), Tony's dad went to get the muffins. When he came back with the muffins, he looked worried.

"The muffins should be golden brown," Tony said. "These muffins don't look done at all!"

"The oven didn't get hot. It must be broken," Tony's dad said.

"What are we going to do?" Tony asked. "The bake sale is in a few hours!"

Tony angrily kicked his football. It rolled across the garden and stopped right in front of a lemon tree. Tony looked up and had an idea.

A few hours later, Tony and his dad were carrying a huge (riesig) cooler of homemade lemonade across the football field. They passed tables filled with cookies, doughnuts, muffins, and cake. The bake sale had already started.

"Oh, thank God you brought some lemonade!" Tony's coach said. "Everybody is so thirsty from all these cookies. Nobody else brought anything to drink."

Everybody wanted to buy a glass of cold lemonade. Soon Tony and his dad ran out of cups. They sold every drop of their wonderful lemonade.

The team earned enough money to buy their uniforms.

(282 words)

_____

_____

_____

_____

_____

_____

_____

_____

_____

_____

Die neue Reihe Kompetent AUFSTEIGEN

✓ Bildungsstandards   ✓ Kompetenzen   ✓ Zentralmatura

Englisch 3
mit Hörverständnis-CD
88 Seiten + 24 Seiten Lösungsheft

In einfachen Merksätzen
und leicht verständlichen
Erklärungen wird der Stoff der
3. Klasse AHS/NMS zusammen-
gefasst. Dazu zählen

- Prepositions
- If-sentences
- Modal verbs
- Revision of tenses
- Listening Comprehensions
- Und vieles mehr ...

Schularbeits-Trainer 3
mit Hörverständnis-CD
44 Seiten + 16 Seiten Lösungsheft

Enthält variantenreiche
Übungstypen in
unterschiedlichen
Schwierigkeitsgraden.
Dazu zählen:

- Fill-in-Übungen
- True-False-Übungen
- Writing Tasks
- Textverständnis-Übungen
- Listening Comprehensions
- Und vieles mehr ...

Die neue Reihe Kompetent AUFSTEIGEN

√ Bildungsstandards √ Kompetenzen √ Zentralmatura

Englisch 4
mit Hörverständnis-CD
88 Seiten + 24 Seiten Lösungsheft

In einfachen Merksätzen
und leicht verständlichen
Erklärungen wird der Stoff der
4. Klasse AHS/NMS zusammen-
gefasst. Dazu zählen

- Comparison
- If-sentences
- ing oder Infinitiv
- Reported speech
- Relative clauses
- Listening Comprehensions
- Und vieles mehr ...

Schularbeits-Trainer 4
mit Hörverständnis-CD
44 Seiten + 12 Seiten Lösungsheft

Enthält variantenreiche
Übungstypen in
unterschiedlichen
Schwierigkeitsgraden.
Dazu zählen:

- Fill-in-Übungen
- True-False-Übungen
- Writing Tasks
- Textverständnis-Übungen
- Listening Comprehensions
- Und vieles mehr ...

Kompetent AUFSTEIGEN gibt es für Mathematik, Englisch und Deutsch!

www.ggverlag.at

G&G

ENGLISCH 3 4
Aufsätze und andere Texte schreiben

Kompetent
AUFSTEIGEN ...

3. und 4. Klasse AHS·NMS

Lösungen

G&G

Describing a person

Raster

body shape: slim, obese, thin, skinny, fat
looks (face, eyes, mouth, hair ...): handsome, old, bald, long, short, big, round, beautiful, pretty, pale, freckled, braid/plait, small, good-looking, curly
clothes: fashionable, old, striped, modern, colourful, old-fashioned
personality: friendly, active, shy, boring, open

Steckbrief

What is the person's name/nickname? Hermione/Minnie
How old is she? 13
How tall is she? tall for her age
What does she look like (body, face, eyes, nose, mouth ...)? long brown hair, green-brown eyes, round face
How does she wear her hair? in a plait/braid
What colour is her hair? brown
What kind of clothes does she usually wear? jeans and T-shirts
Where does she live? in a village in Cornwall, England
Does she have any brothers and/or sisters? twin sister, brother (5)
Does she have any pets? two guinea pigs, dog
What is she good at (at school, outside of school)? Maths, playing piano and playing tennis
What are her hobbies? reading, swimming, riding her bike
Who is her favourite band/singer? Ke$ha
What is her favourite book/movie/TV series? vampire stories, science fiction and fantasy movies, Simpsons
What is her favourite colour? green
What is her favourite food/dish? pizza
What is special about her? friendly, likes to laugh, keeps secrets, good friend

Geordneter und ergänzter Text

My friend is called Melanie but all her friends call her Melli. She is 14 years old. She is not very tall. Melanie has long blonde hair with a few red streaks (Strähnen). She often wears her hair in a ponytail. Melanie is quite slim as she likes doing sports. Melanie has blue eyes and long eyelashes. She hates her lips because she thinks they are too thin.
She often wears skirts and dresses but she also likes to wear jeans. In summer she also wears shorts and sports shoes.
Melli lives in a nice little house with her parents and her two siblings (Geschwister). She goes to school by train as she lives in a small village near Baden. She often goes to the cinema with her older brother and her younger sister. They all love fantasy films.
Melanie loves animals and she has three pets: a rabbit called Arthur, a hamster called Mortimer and a dog called Molly.
When I visit her we sometimes play with her dog Molly. When it is hot we cool off in their swimming pool.
Melli is good at drawing and languages. Her favourite subjects at school are Art, English and Spanish.

Her hobbies are ice skating, reading and playing computer games. Melli likes to read romantic stories but sometimes she also reads books about vampires.

Melanie also plays the saxophone. She does not have a favourite singer or band. Her favourite food is Indian food. Her favourite dessert is apple pie.

Melli is very friendly and she likes meeting new people. In the evening she sometimes chats with her friends on Facebook.

Melli and I often hang out together and whenever I need help she is there for me. She is a really good friend and she never lets me down.

So könnte der Text über Robert aussehen:

My best friend's name is Robert but everybody calls him Robbie.

Robbie is 14 years old and 170 cm tall. He is the tallest boy in our class. Robbie is very thin although he seems to eat all the time. He has short black hair, green eyes and he always looks pale.

Robbie likes to wear jeans and T-shirts and he hates it when he has to wear a shirt and a suit. He feels uncomfortable in elegant clothes.

Robbie lives in Liverpool with his parents and his two younger brothers. They live in a big apartment with a nice little balcony. They have two pets, a cat called Missy and a dog called Tiger. Robbie looks after Tiger and always goes for a walk with him after school.

Robbie is good at soccer and he would like to be a professional football player one day. At school he is really bad at German and Art, so I sometimes help him with his German homework.

Robbie's hobbies are swimming and riding his bike. He is also in the school's swim team. His favourite singer is Justin Bieber, his favourite band are the Black Eyed Peas. Robbie does not really read a lot but he likes to watch action movies. His favourite series is South Park but his parents think it is too violent. Robbie's favourite colour is blue. He loves chocolate cake but he hates cheese.

Robbie is a really good friend. He is very open and you can have a lot of fun with him. When I need help he is always there for me.

(266 words)

Emails

1. Informal or personal emails

Finding mistakes

Dear All,

I **have been** here in Orland Park **for** almost a month now.

On my first day at my new school I was really nervo**u**s because I didn't **know** anybody. I was also a bit worr**ied** about my accent and I was afraid nobody would understand me. But guess what?

There were a lot of other new kids and a friendly teacher helped us find our classes.

My new school is huge and sometimes I still get lost!

School **here** in America is very different from school in **A**ustria. Here the **teachers** stay in the classroom and the kids move around. If you need to go to the toilet (they call it bathroom here) you need a hall pass.

School starts later **than** in Austria but we have to stay at school till 3 p.m. The lessons are only 40 instead of 50 minutes. You can also **choose** some of your classes. I think that is great!

We have the same classes every day. **That's** sometimes boring but I guess I will get used to the new system soon.

After school there are a **lot** of clubs and activiti**es**. I have joined the volleyball team and I sing in the school choir. As my voice is **quite** good I got a part in a musical. I think that's really cool!

The clubs and activities have helped **me** to find **many** new friends.
Of course there are also some bullies at my new school but I try to stay away from them.
Guess what? I have also got one of **these** cool lockers you know from TV! Unfortunately they are not as big as I thought they would be. I was also surprised to see **how** clean the school is. I think they clean the floors with big machines every evening.
Take care and write back soon!
Anna

So könnten deine E-Mails aussehen:

Hi Sabrina,
What are you doing at the weekend? I just checked the cinema programme and found out that they are showing the latest Sandra Bullock movie on Saturday. I would love to go and see it but I don't want to go alone.
Would you like to come with me? I'm sure it will be fun. I'll buy the popcorn this time ☺
CU,
Mimi

Hi Markus,
Just a quick note to let you know that we have arrived safely.
We went straight to our hotel from the airport and after a quick shower and a snack (we didn't get any food on the plane) we got on the tube to Harrod's (It's a good thing we learned how to use the tube map in our English class!). My mum wanted to see the famous Food Halls at Harrod's.
Well, they were okay.
Tomorrow we are going to visit the Tower in the morning and Madam Tussauds in the afternoon. We already got tickets for both places.
For lunch today I had my first fish and chips. I loved it!
London is a very busy place but I think that is cool!
Take care!
Alex

Hi,
HELP! We are going to write a maths test next week but there are still a few things I don't understand. Do you have time to study with me on Sunday and explain the things I don't understand? You know me, I'm terrible at studying alone! I get distracted (abgelenkt) easily.
I'd really appreciate your help! I'll provide the food (loads of muffins) and drinks for us ☺.
Text me on my mobile to let me know if you have time!
Thanks,
Tina

2. Formal emails

Finding mistakes

Dear Mr and Mrs O'Hara,
I **have** now **been** back **for** three weeks but school started a week ago and so it was not possible for **me** to write to you earlier.
How are you? Are you busy as **usual**? Do you have any new guests?
I am **missing** you and all my friends from the language school a **lot**! We had so much fun together!

Thank you for treating me **like** a member of your family.

How is Misty, my favourite dog? Does he still try to steal **any** food that you don't put away but **leave** on the kitchen table?

Last week I **got an** email from my Italian friend Guilia (**Remember** Guilia ? She stayed with your neighbours.). Like me she is still in contact with some of the boys and girls from my language class. I was lucky because I made so **many** good friends **while** I was in England. It was really interesting to meet **people** from all over the world. As I had to speak a lot of **E**nglish I think my spoken English has improved a lot (unfortunately I still have problems with my written English).

My parents, my brother and my sister are all fine. My sister will take her A-level exams this year, so we are all very **excited**. My brother is still crazy about football and he is now playing in a football team! My mum is wor**ried** that he **will not have** enough time to study for school!

By the way, I think I left a **pair of jeans** and a T-shirt in the cupboard of my room. Could you please send them to me? Please let us know **how** much money you **paid** for shipping my clothes.

Please write soon. My parents send **their** regards. I hope I can come back again next year. I really loved staying with you. Thank you for **everything**! I hope there are not **too** many mistakes in this letter.

Yours sincerely,

Thomas

So könnten deine E-Mails aussehen:

Dear Dr White,

I am writing to you because I need your advice.

I turned 14 two weeks ago but my parents still do not want to let me stay out longer than 9 p.m., not even at weekends. All my friends are all allowed to stay out till 11 p.m. or later!

When I tried to talk to my parents they just said that I am still too young to go to youth clubs or discos. They are afraid that I will start drinking or get into contact with drugs.

How can I convince them that I am not going to get into trouble and that they cannot protect me forever?

Yours sincerely,

Zoe

Email of application

Emily Jackson
Hauptplatz 5
5340 St. Gilgen

Martina Freitag
Rosengasse 23
2542 Kottingbrunn

4th March, 20..

Dear Ms Jackson,

I saw your advertisement in our local paper and I would like to apply for the job. I am 16 years old and I would love to work at your English summer camp. It would be a great opportunity to earn some money and practice my English at the same time.

I have a lot of experience with children as I have three younger brothers and sisters. They are 3, 6 and 11. I often help my parents to look after them. I also play with them or help them with their homework.

I also have some experience as a babysitter. I have worked for families in our neighbourhood, looking after kids who range in age from 1 to 10.

I have been learning English for 6 years, so my command of English is quite good. I regularly go to

England with my parents in the summer. Last year I even attended a summer course in Brighton. If you need any references, my English teacher would be more than happy to provide them. I hope you will consider my application and I look forward to hearing from you.

Yours sincerely,
Martina Freitag

Continue the story

Deine Geschichte könnte so aussehen:

When Peter looked out of the window he couldn't believe his eyes. There was a strange object right in front of his window. It was yellow and green and looked like a miniature spaceship. "What the heck is this?" he thought. "Sandy, come here! Look!" he shouted. Sandy, Peter's sister, stormed into the room. "What is it?" she asked. "Look outside," Peter answered. Now Sandy saw the yellow and green object in the garden too. "Do you think what I think it is?" she asked. Peter didn't answer. He kept staring out of the window. "Maybe we should go and take a closer look at it," Sandy said. Together they went out into the garden. As they were alone at home they were scared but at the same time they wanted to know what the strange object really was.
Suddenly a small door on the miniature spaceship opened and a tiny creature stepped out.
Sandy and Peter were really excited. A real alien had landed in their garden! It did not look like any of the aliens in the movies Sandy and Peter liked to watch. It almost looked like a human being, only much shorter.
Before the two children could say anything they heard a kind of voice in their heads. Did the strange creature use telepathy to communicate with them? Somehow they could understand what the visitor from outer space was trying to tell them. He was from a far away planet called Xerox 3 and on the way to a planet called Xenia 5 his spaceship had broken down. That's why he had landed in Sandy's and Peter's garden. He asked the children for some tools because he needed to repair his spaceship. He could only stay on the earth for a few hours as the oxygen (Sauerstoff) in the air was bad for him.
Peter and Sandy helped their strange guest to repair his spaceship. They had many questions but they understood that he had to leave as quickly as possible if he did not want to die.
After three hours the man from outer space said goodbye to Peter and Sandy and then he took off in his spaceship again.
"I hope he will come back one day!" Sandy said and then she and Peter went back into the house.

(335 words)

Writing a story from prompts

Deine Geschichte könnte so aussehen:

camping holiday in Australia, bush fire, tent, get lost, scared, kangaroo, rescue plane, happy

Tom, Sally and Peter were good friends. They were students at Barchester University and spent a lot of time together.
Last year they decided to go on a camping holiday in Australia. None of them had ever been to Australia, but they were all very interested in the nature of this continent and in the culture of the Aborigines, the native people of Australia.

Then the big day arrived and they boarded a plane to Sydney. There they rented a car and started their trip into the outback. The weather was very hot and dry. After a long drive and a night in a tiny hotel, they reached an area where hardly anyone lived.

In the evening they put up their tents and spent the first night in the Australian outback.

On the next day they drove on and Sally was very excited because she was the first one to spot a kangaroo right next to the road. While they were driving and listening to the news on the radio they heard that there was a big bush fire not far from where they were. "Maybe we should go back," Tom said. "I've heard these fires are really dangerous!" "Don't be stupid," Peter said and drove on. But suddenly there was a strong wind and on their left they saw something like a firewall coming closer and closer. The bushland was on fire and suddenly there was smoke everywhere. "We have to get away from here!" Sally shouted. "Turn right!" So Peter left the road and drove into the bush.

Soon they were lost. The three friends were very scared but they knew they had to drive on to get away from the fire.

Fortunately they had a mobile phone that worked in the wilderness. They called the rangers but could not tell them where they were. So the rangers sent a rescue plane to look for the three young people. After some time the pilot saw their car and found a place where he could land the plane. Tom, Sally and Peter got onto the plane and a ranger drove their car back to the next town. The young people were happy that they had survived the bush fire.

Adventure/Mystery/Fantasy stories

So könnte deine Geschichte aussehen:

Peter and Tim were best friends although they were very different.

Peter loved reading, he was a clever boy who always helped his friends when they had a problem. There was just one thing Peter was not good at – sports.

Tim was very good at sports, he was tall and strong and when he wanted to achieve (erreichen) something he never gave up. He also loved animals, most of all, his dog Rusty. There was just one thing Tim was not good at – remembering things.

One day the two friends wanted to watch birds on Mount Elsie, a small mountain near their hometown. They set out early in the morning and enjoyed the walk in the bright sunshine. When they were already quite high up and were just watching a beautiful falcon (Falke) the weather suddenly changed. The sky was cloudy and all of a sudden there was fog everywhere. The boys could hardly see their hands in front of their faces. They could not see the path (Pfad) that would take them back home. They had no idea where they were.

"Let's take the compass, it will help us to find the way back," Peter said.

"The compass? Oh no, I forgot to put it into my backpack!" Tim answered.

Peter could not believe it. Now he was really angry with Tim.

"I'm sure we can find the way without a compass," Tim said. "Let's go!"

Without looking back he started to climb down the mountain.

"Stop!" Peter shouted. "This is much too dangerous! Let's stay here and call our parents on the mobile phone."

"Don't be childish, you are such a coward!" Tim answered and disappeared in the fog.

Peter couldn't understand his friend. He called his parents and told them everything. They phoned the mountain rangers who soon found Peter. Then they started looking for Tim. When they found him he was lying on the ground because he had fallen and sprained his ankle.

The mountain rangers took the two boys back to their parents. Peter was glad that nothing worse had happened to his friend. Tim had to see a doctor and had to wear a bandage on his leg for a few days. Both boys were very happy to be back home.

8

Fairy tale

Part 1
The three magic nuts
Once upon a time there was a poor family. The farmer and his wife had three sons and a daughter.
The daughter was called Happy because she was friendly and always made her brothers laugh.
One day the father said, "All our money is gone and we have nothing to eat. I have to go to the castle
and try to find work. Maybe the king needs a hunter."
Happy's three brothers went with their father. They hoped that they would also find work at the castle.
While her father and her brothers were gone Happy went into the wood to collect firewood.
Suddenly she saw something shining in the grass. When she went closer she saw that the shining
thing was a golden nut. When she picked it up she saw two more golden nuts lying in the grass.
Happy could not believe her luck. She took the nuts and ran home.
She showed the nuts to her mother. At first they did not know what to do with the nuts. Then Happy
had an idea. "Maybe they are magic nuts. Let's open them and see what is inside."

Part 2
1c / 2f / 3g / 4b / 5d / 6e / 7a

When Happy opened the first nut she suddenly heard a voice: "Eat the nut, then make a wish."
Happy was really excited. The nuts were indeed magic!
First Happy wanted a nice house for her family and herself, then she wanted enough food for all of
them. When eating the third nut she asked for happiness.
When Happy's father and brothers came home they were very tired and sad because they had not
found any work at the castle. When they came to the place where their old house had been they
could not believe their eyes. What had happened?
Happy told them about the three magic nuts and what she had wished for. They thanked her because
now they had a nice house, enough food, and they were happy.
When the neighbour found out about the three magic nuts he was really angry. He thought that he
would have made better use of the nuts. He decided to go into the wood too. Maybe he would also
find some magic nuts.
Well, he did indeed find three magic nuts! When he came home he opened them, ate them and made
his wishes: He wanted to live in a palace, he wanted to be rich, and he wanted to be powerful.
When he lived in his palace he felt very lonely. He also had money but he did not know who he could
trust. He also had power but he did not have a lot of friends. He was very unhappy.
The farmer and his family, on the other hand, had made good wishes and they lived happily ever after.

Summary

So könnte deine Zusammenfassung aussehen:

Summary of "The story of St. Patrick"
St. Patrick, who is the patron saint of Ireland, was born in Wales at the end of the 4th century. As a
teenager he had to work as a slave on a farm in Ireland. He managed to escape and went back to
Wales where he decided to become a priest. Later he returned to Ireland and brought Christianity to
this country. A legend says that there are no snakes in Ireland because St. Patrick drove them into the
sea with a wooden stick.
Today Irish people all over the world celebrate St. Patrick's Day on March 17th.

(105 words)